Louis Molpoer

Every Lady her own Dressmaker

The scientific Lady Tailor System for cutting Ladies' Dresses and Coats

Louis Molpoer

Every Lady her own Dressmaker
The scientific Lady Tailor System for cutting Ladies' Dresses and Coats

ISBN/EAN: 9783337122812

Printed in Europe, USA, Canada, Australia, Japan

Cover: Foto ©ninafisch / pixelio.de

More available books at **www.hansebooks.com**

◁ PRICE, $5.00 ▷

EVERY LADY HER OWN DRESSMAKER.

— •

THE SCIENTIFIC

LADY TAILOR SYSTEM

FOR

CUTTING LADIES' DRESSES AND COATS.

NO FITTING TO DO.

IMPROVED AND SIMPLIFIED

——•——

SECOND EDITION.

— •

AS TAUGHT BY

◁ **PROF. LOUIS MOLPOER** ▷

WASHINGTON, D. C.

Important Notice.

No person shall have any right. whatever, to use in any manner my Scientific Lady Tailor System without having first procured from me, or my authorized agent, a book signed by me.

Entered according to act of Congress. on the fifth day of March, 1891. by Louis Molfoer. in the office of the Librarian of Congress. at Washington. D. C. No. of copyright, 8375.

———

This is to Certify, *That M*

has the right to use my Improved System of Dress Cutting. for which has been paid the sum of $5.00.

Teaching

———

I agree to use the said system for my own use only, and will not teach it to any one without the written consent of the owner. or a duly authorized agent.

Rules for Basting.

A basting thread must be run on the line of the waist.

Baste carefully, that lining and outside are perfectly smooth.

In basting up the waist, pin at the waist and arm lines, and hold long seam next to you. The most troublesome seam in the whole waist is the curved side body seam, which comes next to the back. In basting this seam on one side of the back commence at the waist line and go up as in other seams, holding the outward curved seam toward you. The other side must be pinned at the waist line, and at intervals up the seam, then commence basting at the top, holding the outward curved seam toward you, as on the other side.

In sewing up seams do not have the machine stitch too short, or it will draw.

Nick the seams, so that the waist will spring nicely into the figure, and then press them all open. If you wish to finish with tailor-like neatness, bind the seams with ribbon.

No hook and eye pieces are required, but instead a waist-band should be put inside the dress to keep it in place.

All seams must be allowed. One-half inch is enough, except under the arms, where the seams should be somewhat deeper. It is absolutely necessary to use a tracing wheel in order to have your lines perfectly true.

After the dress is well cut, it must be made with great care, paying strict attention to the rules.

In cutting velvet, the nap must be run up; in plush like-wise; in sealskin, down.

In cutting plaid be sure to match the stripes in waist, skirt and trimming, which can always be done.

If the silesia, drilling, or other material used for lining the waist, is cut crossways it is less apt to stretch. It is economy to use a good quality of material for lining, as a poor lining will wear out sooner than outside goods, and the result will be that the seam will stretch, and the waist lose its shape.

A dress should not be made so tight as to draw. The corset should be pulled in as required, and the waist should be fitted over it easily and without wrinkles. The seams will stretch and fray out if this rule is not followed. The same corset should be worn with the dress it was measured and fitted over, as different corsets change the figure. A dressmaker should make it a rule never to measure a lady over old or ill-fitting corsets.

The Purpose of This Book.

This book is intended to explain the principles of Dress Cutting, and is founded on systematic rules, by which any one can learn to measure, draft, baste, cut, fit and make dresses without further instruction.

To Dressmakers.—It will be of great use to the professional dressmakers, who, like the inventor, have had the same sad experience in the use of all other charts and systems.

To Ladies in Private Life.—It is especially adapted to the use of those ladies who wish to alter or make their own dresses for home and morning wear. It is as much trouble or more to a dressmaker to make a chintz or percale dress, as one of more expensive material; yet few ladies are willing to pay as much, for it is probable that the making would often be three times as much as the original cost. If this class of work be done by the ladies themselves, or if they choose to superintend it at home, professional dressmakers will have more time to devote to the finer or more artistic work.

To Young Ladies.—Young ladies, to you this book and the system it teaches will be valuable. Many of you object to spending at least six to eight months' time in learning the trade. Most of those who do this are but wasting their time. There are few who are taught the art of measuring, drafting, or cutting by rule, basting and fitting, and that all seams are put together differently; some having to be stretched, while others should be held in. In fact, we have known dressmakers who never allowed their apprentices to get a glimpse of these necessary things, but kept them continually employed in one special branch, such as quilling, ruffling, fluting, button-hole making, overcasting, etc.

The time has now come when a young lady's education will be considered unfinished unless she is an adept in this art.

We guarantee perfect Arm Holes, Sleeves, Busts. Darts, Curves and Neck without Refitting. It is simply perfect in all its simplicity and beauty, and we are pleased to cut any one Test Dress to Prove its Merits.

Never take instructions in any system without having Test Dress cut and tried on. Many claim to be self-fitting, but judge for yourself whether the fit is good or bad.

We have tried all these so-called Tailor Systems. and do not wonder that experienced dressmakers are disgusted with them. Practice and experience enable us to say that we have yet to record a single failure in the use of our New system.

It is our experience and the basis of our system, that without a perfect arm hole it is impossible to have perfect fitting waist and sleeves.

Our system is the only one by which a perfect sleeve can be made without a particle of alteration. The rules are so plain both for measuring and drafting. that with ordinary care a mistake is almost impossible.

Many will inquire, "What is the difference between the SCIENTIFIC LADY TAILOR SYSTEM, and the other so-called Tailor Systems?" Taught from pasteboard. with imitation square attached, which are only a deception and fraud, as no person will ever be able to use a square without the attachment.

By learning the SCIENTIFIC LADY TAILOR SYSTEM. you will be competent to cut like a tailor, by the tape measure alone, designated from any fashion plate. either English. French or American styles. This can be learned in a very short time; a few hours will instruct a dressmaker without refitting or the use of any pattern.

Measure for Drafting Basque.

1.	Waist. - - - - - - -	22 inches
2.	Under Arm. - - - - - -	8 "
3.	Arm Eye. - - - - - -	14½ "
4.	Width of Back. - - - -	12 "
5.	Length of Back. - - - -	14 x 14 "
6.	Neck, - - - - - -	13 "
7.	Bust. - - - - - -	36 "
8.	Length of Front. - - -	13½ "
9.	Width of Chest. - - - -	12 "
10.	Height of Dart, - - -	5½ "
11.	Height of Hip. - - - -	4 "
12.	Around Hip. - - - -	36 "
13.	Shoulder, - - - -	4½ "
14.	Neck to Elbow. - - -	19½ "
15.	Inside to Bend. - - -	8 "
16.	Inside to Wrist. - - -	16 "
17.	Upper Arm. - - - -	12 "
18.	Middle. - - - - -	11 "
19.	Elbow. - - - - -	11 "
20.	Lower Arm. - - - -	10 "
21.	Wrist. - - - - -	8 "

Directions for Taking Measures.

1. *Waist Measure.*—Draw tape tight around the waist.

2. *Under Arm.*—First put on the belt, and then measure from the bottom of the belt to close under the arm.

3. *Arm Eye.*—Place tape under the arm and draw tape up over end of shoulder.

4. *Width of Back.*—From arm to arm.

5. *Length of Back.*—From the bone of the neck to the bottom of the belt, and if the lady is long waisted there is an extension below the belt varying from one to one and one-fourth inches, which should always be added to the length of back below line 1.

6. *Neck Measure.*—Place the tape around the neck, close over the inside collar.

7. *Bust Measure.*—Place the tape around the fullest part of the bust up over the shoulder blades closely.

8. *Length of Front.*—Front hollow in the neck to lower part of belt.

9. *Chest Measure.*—From shoulder to shoulder across the chest.

10. *Height of Dart.*—From the bottom of the belt up.

11. *Height of Hip.*—From the belt down to the hip bone.

12. *Hip Measure.*—Around the hip over the bustle.

13. *Shoulder Measure.*—From the neck to end of shoulder.

14. *Neck to Elbow Measure.*—Place the hand to the neck before measuring, then pass the tape from the neck over point of shoulder to the point of elbow.

15. *Inside Measure to the Bend of the Arm.*—Place the tape close up under the arm and measure to the inside bend of the elbow.

16. *Inside Measure to Wrist.*—While you have the tape as in direction 15, bring tape on down to the wrist, and note both measures.

17. *Upper Arm Measure.*—Around the arm. The same for middle and lower arm measures, keeping the arm bent so the muscles will expand.

18. *Elbow Measure.*—Place the tape around the elbow when the arm is straight, then bend the arm, keeping the tape over the point of the elbow.

19. *Wrist Measure.*—Place the tape around the hand over the thumb, so the sleeve will be just large enough for the hand to slip through.

20. *Skirt Measure.*—Place the tape at the bottom of the belt and bring down to the top of the right foot, which is placed out, while the lady stands upright. The back should be two inches longer if bustle is wanted. Skirt should vary in width according to the size of the wearer, from two and one-eighth yards to two and one-half. Two and one-eighth for a medium sized lady.

— •

Always Use a Belt.

Never take a measure without using a belt, as you are likely to take back length too long, which will cause wrinkles on the hips and too much length between arm and neck. Strictly observe all rules in the book and we guarantee a fit without alteration.

The use of curvatures is to get even lines ; unless you do this your seams will not be straight, which causes wrinkles. There are a very few who are able to curve without the aid of curvatures.

Draw straight lines,   -   -   -   -
Curve even seams.   -   -   -   -
Trace in the lines,   -   -   -   -
Stitch straight.   -   -   -   -
Press seams open. -   -   -   -   -

BASQUE No. 1.

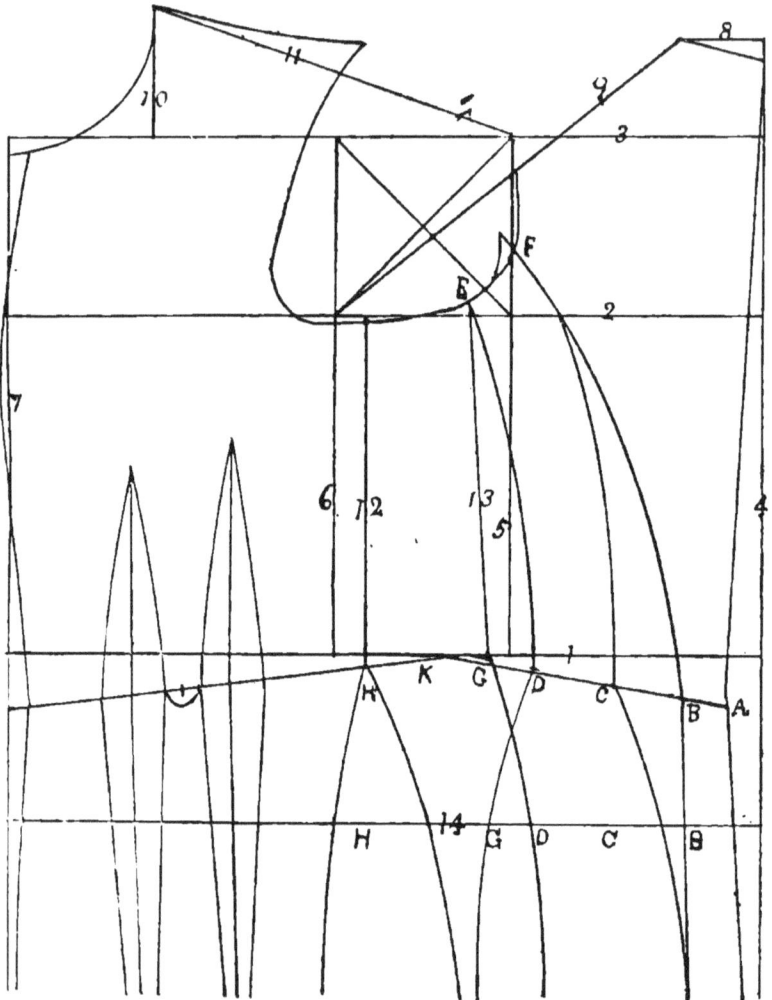

Directions for Basque No. 1.

1. Draw line 1 eight inches from the bottom of the paper for belt line.

2. Draw line 2 the height of under arm measure above line 1.

3. Draw line 3 the diameter of arm eye measure above line 2.

4. Draw line 4 the length of back above line 1, one inch from the edge of the paper to the right and add the extension below line 1.

5. Dot to the left of line 4, on lines 1 and 3, half the width of the back, and draw line 5 through dots just made, from line 3 to line 1.

6. Dot to the left of line 5, on lines 1 and 3, the diameter of the arm eye measure and draw line 6 through the dots just made from line 3 to line 1.

7. Dot on lines 1 and 3, to the left of line 4, half the bust measure, and draw line 7 through dots just made from line 3 down the whole length of front.

8. Draw slanting diameter of square, by drawing a cross mark from the junction of lines 3 and 5, and 3 and 6.

9. Draw line 8 to the left of line 4, one-sixth of the neck measure, for back of the neck.

10. Draw line 9 from the end of line 8 to the junction of lines 2 and 6, for back shoulder line.

11. Dot A is one inch to the left of the end of line 4, below line 1, and draw a line from junction lines 8 and 4 to dot A.

12. Take half the space between 5 and 6, on line 1, and make dot K, draw slanting waist line from dot A to K and draw to the end of line 7.

13.   Dot to the right of line 7 on line 3. one-fourth the neck measure and draw line 10 up from dot just made on line 3, one-half of an inch less for front of neck. and use neck curvature from the end of line 10 to one-half of an inch below line 3 to line 7.

14.   Draw line 11 from top of neck to junction of 3 and 5.

15.   Place the end of the rule at the top of neck. letting it cross center of the square and measure from the top of the neck for shoulder and make a dot the length of the shoulder.

16.   To the right of line 7. one and one-half inches above line 2. take half the chest measure and make a dot where half the chest measure comes.

17.   To curve the arm eye. first take half the space between lines 9 and 2 on line 5 and make dot F. and then curve from the junction of lines 9 and 5 to dot F. and then round to half the space between lines 5 and 6 on line 2 and then up through the chest measure and up to shoulder measure and above line 11. the height of arm eye measure, then measure the back shoulder line, and make the front shoulder one-quarter of an inch shorter, and curve from the top of the arm eye to top of the neck.

18.   One inch to the left of dot A, make dot B. take half the space between dot A and line 5 on waist line and make dot C. Dot D is one-half inch to the right of line 5 on waist line. Dot E is one-half inch to the left of slanting diameter to the right in arm eye.

19.   Place large end of curvature at dot B and draw a curved line to one-fourth of an inch above dot F. and curve down to half the space between dot F and E in arm eye ; for inside of back. use curvature the same way from dot C, letting it touch back line at line 2 for outside of side body.

20.   Use the curvature the same way from dot D to dot E for inside of side body.

21. Measure the space between lines 6 and 7 on slanting waist line, for darts, in four equal parts. The space between darts is found by measuring three-eighths of an inch on each side of the center mark.

22. Draw a line in each center of space for darts, front dart according to measure, and back dart one-fourth inch higher. and slanting back one-fourth inch, then curve for darts by placing the small end of curvature on the end of each line and curve to waist line.

23. Curve the back of neck from end of line 9 to one-half inch below line 8 on line 4, then measure back neck and front neck to half of neck measure and make a (dot.) Curve front of waist from this dot one-half inch above line 2, make rounding curve and into height of dart and into waist line one-half inch. and out to line 7 at bottom of paper.

24. To find the back line of the front and under arm gore, measure from D to C for side body, and from B to A for back. omitting the space between B and C, and then from the front curved line to front dart. omitting the width of darts, measure the space between the darts and from the back dart to half the waist measure and make dot G. If G comes to the right of line 5 then use rule 24 of No. 2 Basque, if not measure half the space between G and back dart and make dot H.

25. Draw line 12 from H up to arm eye straight for back of front and front of under arm gore, and draw line 13 from G to E for back of under arm gore.

26. Extend lines 4 and 7 to the bottom of paper and center lines of darts, slanting back one-fourth inch, also outside lines of darts. leaving one-half inch each side the center lines at the bottom of paper.

27. Measure for hip line on lines 7 and 4 ; from line 1 the height of hip and draw line 14 for hip line. Mark C. D, G and H on hip line, exactly below letters on waist line.

28. Draw back line from A to one-half inch to the left of end of line 4 at bottom of paper with rule.

29. Draw inside of back from B straight down to bottom of paper with rule.

30. Back of the side body is sloped from C one inch to the right of C on hip line with curvature.

31. Front of side body is sloped from D one inch to the left of D on hip line.

32. Back of under arm gore is sloped from G one inch to the right of G on hip line.

33. Front of under arm gore is sloped from H one inch to the left of H on hip line.

34. Back of front is sloped from H one and one-fourth inches to the right of H on hip line.

35. If too large or too small after measuring all the places on hip line, add on or take off to suit the hip measure.

P. S.—Always baste the sleeves in, and the collar on, before putting on the garment.

To Draft the Measure of Arm Eye.

6	inches in	circumference	gives	a diameter of	2	inches.
7	"	"	"	"	2¼	"
8	"	"	"	"	2½	"
9	"	"	"	"	3	"
10	"	"	"	"	3¼	"
11	"	"	"	"	3½	"
12	"	"	"	"	3¾	"
13	"	"	"	"	4	"
14	"	"	"	"	4¼	"
15	"	"	"	"	4½	"
16	"	"	"	"	4¾	"
17	"	"	"	"	5	"
18	"	"	"	"	5¼	"
19	"	"	"	"	5½	"
20	"	"	"	"	5¾	"

☞ Take particular care not to get diameter too large.

BASQUE No. 2.

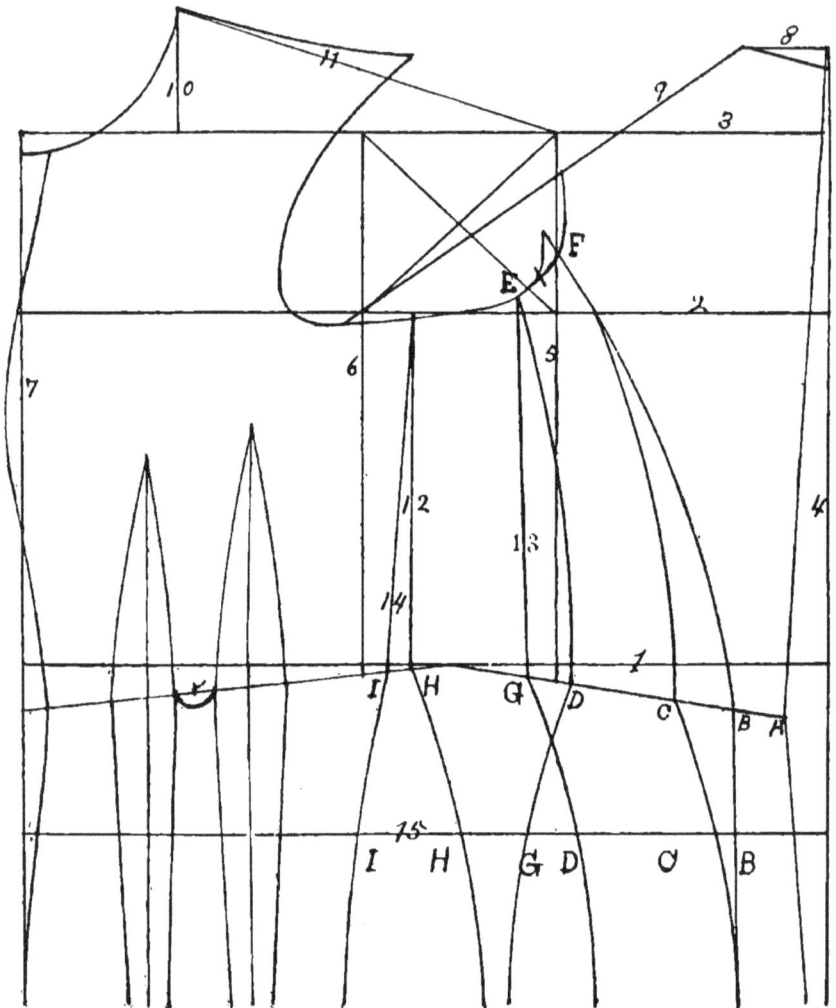

Directions for Basque No. 2.

Proceed as in Basque No. 1 until you get to rule 24.

24.   One inch to the left of dot K, on waist line, make dot II, and draw line 12 from II up to arm eye straight for back of front; then measure side body, back and front, and take the remainder of the waist measure; put one half to the right of K and make dot G, the other half to the left of K on waist line and make dot I; draw line 13 from G to E for back of under arm gore, draw line 14 from I up to top of line 12 for front of under arm gore.

25.   Extend lines 4 and 7 to the bottom of paper and center lines of darts, slanting back one-fourth inch, also outside lines of darts, leaving one-half inch each side the center lines at the bottom of paper.

26.   Measure for hip line on lines 7 and 4 from line 1, the height of hip, and draw line 15 for hip line.   Mark C, D, G, II and I on hip line, exactly below letters on waist line.

27.   Draw back line from A to one-half inch to the left of end of line 4 at bottom of paper with rule.

28.   Draw inside of back from B straight down to bottom of paper with rule.

29.   Back of the side body is sloped from C one inch to the right of C on hip line.

30.   Front of side body is sloped from D one inch to the left of D on hip line.

31.   Back of under arm gore is sloped from G one inch to the right of G on hip line.

32.   Front of under arm gore is sloped from I three-fourths of an inch to the left of I on hip line.

33.   Back of front is sloped from II one and one-fourth inches to the right of II on hip line.

34.   If too large or too small after measuring all the places on hip line, add on or take off to suit the hip measure.

BASQUE FOR FRENCH BIAS DART.

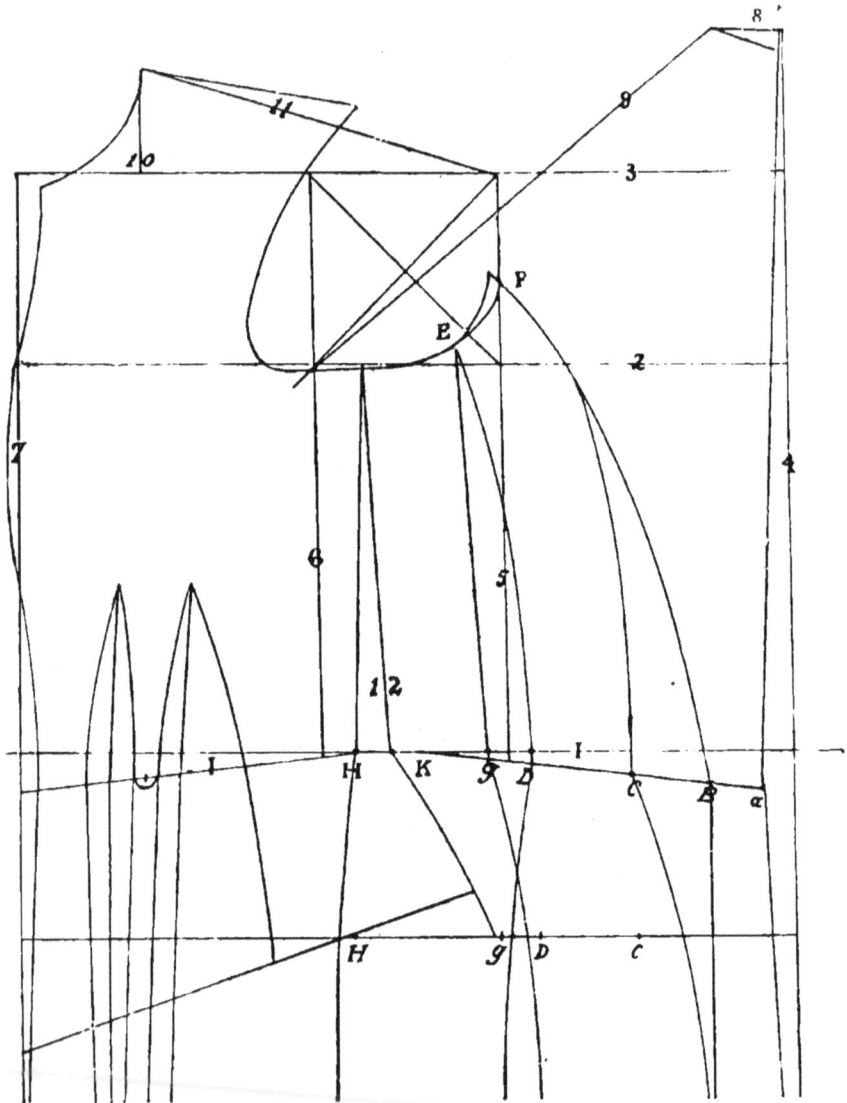

French Bias Dart.

Proceed as in Basque No. 1 until you get to rule 21.

21.   To the right of line 7, on waist line take half the chest measure and make a dot, divide the space between this dot and line 7 into four equal parts for darts.   Curve the darts the same as in plain basque with the exception of curving the back of the back dart. which is curved through the chest measure to four inches below the waist line.

22.   Curve the front of the waist the same as in basque No. 1.

23.   Three-fourth inch to the left of line 5 make dot G and three inches to the left of dot G make dot H, on waist line; draw a line from H up to arm eye straight for front of under arm gore. and draw line 13 from G to E for back of under arm gore.

24.   Then measure from H to G for under arm gore. and from D to C for side body, from B to A for back. and from front curved line to dart. space between the darts and from back bias dart to half the waist measure and make a dot. Place the small end of curvature to the top of line H and curve down to half the waist measure, dot on waist line for line 12, which makes the back of the front.

P. S.—Half the waist measure (dot) should come within one-quarter inch either to right or left of K. if not make under arm gore larger or smaller.

25.   Extend lines 4 and 7 to the bottom of the paper. and centre lines of darts and outside lines of front dart and left side of back dart to three-eighths of an inch from centre lines at bottom of paper.

26.   Measure for hip line on lines 4 and 7 the height of hip. below line 1, and draw line 14 for hip line. Mark C. D. G and H on hip line exactly below letters on waist line.

27. Draw outside of back from A to down one-half inch to the left of line 4 at bottom of the paper with rule.

28. Draw inside of back from B straight down to bottom of paper with rule.

29. Back of side body is sloped from C one inch to the right of C on hip line with curvature.

30. Front of side body is sloped from D one inch to the left of D on hip line.

31. Back of under arm gore is sloped from G to one inch to the right of G on hip line.

32. Front of under arm gore is sloped from H one-half inch to the left of H on hip line.

33. Then measure under arm gore. side body and back and from front curved line to the dart space between the darts and from back bias dart to half the hip measure and make a dot on hip line. Curve from line 12 on waist line to this dot on hip line for back of front.

Rules for Two Under Arm Gores—Bias Dart.

Proceed as in basque for French Bias Dart until you get to under arm gores.

1. Take width of side body and one-half inch to the right of dot K and make dot G on waist line and dot I to the left of dot G the width of side body, and draw line 14 from I up to arm eye straight for front of front under arm gore and draw line 13 from G up to half the space between dot E and top of line 14 in arm eye for back of front under arm gore.

2. Again take width of side body and one-half inch to left of dot K, make dot L and dot N to the right of L the width of side body and draw line 15 from L up to top of line 13 in arm eye for front of back under arm gore. Draw line 16 from N to dot E for back of back under arm gore.

3. Measure from I to G and from L to N for under arm gores, and then from D to C for side body, and from B to A for back, and from front curved line to dart space between darts, and from back bias dart to half the waist measure and make a dot. Use small end of curvature from top of line 14 to dot just made on waist line for back of front, which makes line 12.

4. Proceed for hip measure as in basque above with the exception of under arm gores which are curved one-half inch to right and left of letters on hip line. Measure under arm gores, side body, back from front curved line to dart, space between the darts from the back bias dart to half the hip measure and make a dot on hip line, and curve from end of line 12 on waist line to dot just made on hip line for back of front.

BASQUE FOR TWO UNDER ARM GORES.

COPYRIGHTED.

Basque for Two Under Arm Gores.

Proceed as in Basque No. 1 until you get to rule 24.

24.   One and one-half inches to the left of dot K make dot H, and draw line 12 from dot H up to arm eye straight for back of front, then measure side body back and front; take half of the remainder of the waist measure and put equally to the right of K and make dot G, and to the left of dot H make dot I, and draw line 13 from dot G up to half the space between dot E and end of line 12 in arm eye, and draw line 14 from dot I to top of line 12, which makes front under arm gore, and then take the remaining portion of waist measure and one-half inch to the left of dot K make dot L and dot N to the right where the remainder of the waist measure comes, and draw line 16 from dot N to dot E, and draw line 15 from dot L up to top of line 13, which makes back under arm gore.

25.   Extend lines 4 and 7 to the bottom of paper and centre lines of darts, slanting back one-fourth inch, also outside lines of darts, leaving one-half inch each side the centre lines at the bottom of paper.

26.   Measure for hip line on lines 7 and 4 from line 1, the height of hip, and draw line 17 for hip line.   Mark C, D. N, G, L, H and I on hip line, exactly below letters on waist line.

27.   Draw back line from A to one-half inch to the left of end of line 4 at bottom of paper with rule.

28.   Draw inside of back from B straight down to bottom of paper with rule.

29.   Back of the side body is sloped from C one inch to the right of C on hip line.

30.   Front of side body is sloped from D one inch to the left of D on hip line.

31.   Back of back under arm gore is sloped from N to one-half inch to the right of **N** on hip line.   Front of back under arm gore is sloped from L to one-half inch to the left of **L** on hip line.

32.   Back of front under arm gore is sloped from G to one-half inch to the right of G on hip line.   Front of front under arm gore is sloped from I to one-half inch to the left of I on hip line.

33.   Back of the front is sloped from H one and one-fourth inch to the right of H on hip line.

PRINCESS OR POLONAISE.

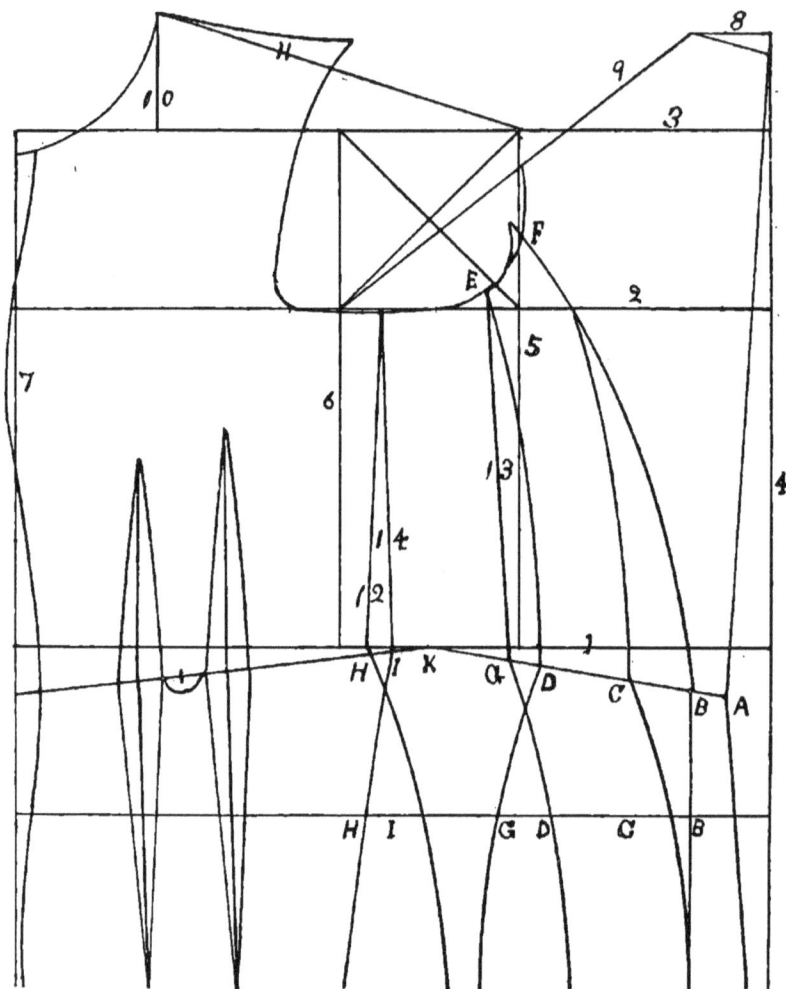

Princess or Polonaise.

Proceed as in Basque No. 1. until you get to Rule 22.

22. Draw a line in each center of space for darts, after taking out one-fourth of each dart from the outside of darts, and draw front dart according to measure, and back dart one-quarter inch higher, and slanting back one-fourth inch, then curve for darts by placing the small end of long curvature on the end of each line and curve to waist line.

23. Curve the back of neck from end of line 9 to one-half inch below line 8 on line 4, then measure back neck and front neck to half of neck measure and make a (dot.) Curve front of waist from this dot one-half inch above line 2. make rounding curve and into height of dart and into waist line one-half inch, and out to line 7 at bottom of paper.

24. Then measure the side body and back. and from front curved line to dart, omitting the space of darts, and measure the space between darts. and then from back dart to half the waist measure and make a dot. Take half the space from dot just made and back dart and make dot II. and draw line 12 from 11 up to the arm eye for back of front, slanting a little to the right. Then take the space of the darts you have taken out and put to the right of 11 on waist line, and make dot 1. and put the same space to the right of half the waist measure dot, and make dot G. and draw line 13 from G to E for back of under arm gore; draw line 14 from I up to end of line 12 in arm eye for front of under arm gore.

P. S.—If half the waist measure comes to the right of line 5, proceed the same as in Basque No. 2. with the exception of drawing the center and outside lines of darts together at bottom of paper.

25. Extend lines 4 and 7 to the bottom of paper and center lines of darts, slanting back one-half inch. also outside lines of darts, letting them touch center lines at bottom of paper.

26.   Measure for hip line on lines 7 and 4; from line 1 the height of hip and draw line 15 for hip line.   Mark C. D. G, I and H on hip line, exactly below letters on waist line.

27.   Draw back line from A to one-half inch to the left of end of line 4 at bottom of paper with rule.

28.   Draw inside of back from B straight down to bottom of paper with rule.

29.   Back of the side body is sloped from C one inch to the right of C on hip line.

30.   Front of side body is sloped from D one inch to the left of D on hip line.

31.   Back of under arm gore is sloped from G one inch to the right of G on hip line.

32.   Front of under arm gore is sloped from I three-fourths an inch to the left of I on hip line.

33.   Back of the front is sloped from H one and one-fourth inch to the right of H on hip line.

34.   If too large or too small after measuring all the places on hip line, add on or take off to suit the hip measure.

SLEEVE No. 1.
COPYRIGHTED.

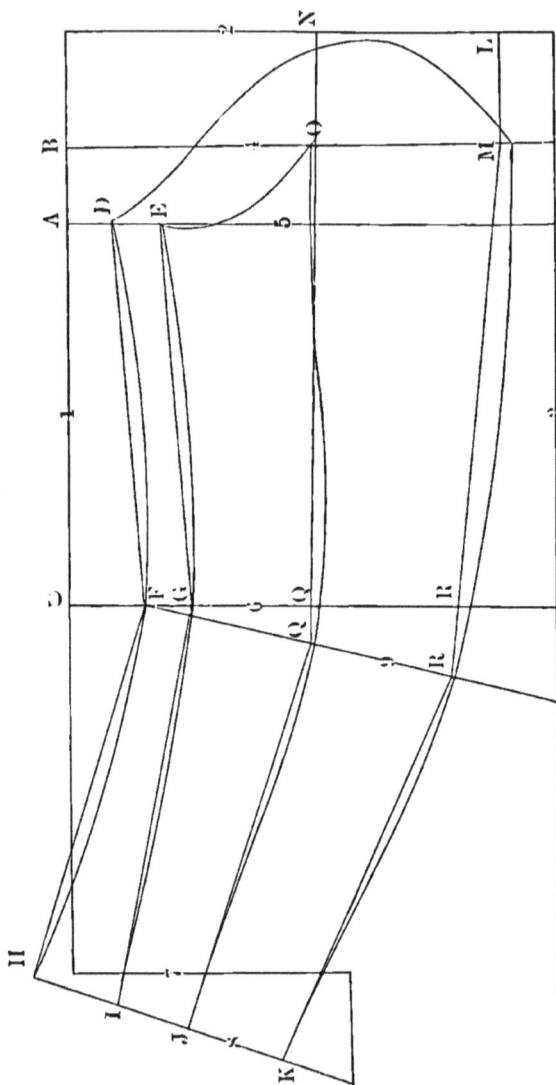

Measure for Drafting Sleeve.

1.—Arm Eye . . . . 14 inches	6.—Upper Arm . . . . 12 inches
2.—Neck to Elbow . . . . . 19½ inches	7.—Middle Arm . . . . . . 11 inches
3.—Shoulder . . . . 4½ inches	8.—Elbow . . . . 11 inches
4.—Inside to Bend . . . . . 8 inches	9.—Lower Arm . . . . . . 10 inches
5.—Inside to Wrist . . . . 16 inches	10.—Wrist . . . . 8 inches

Rules for Drafting Sleeve No. 1.

1. Line 1 is the diameter of arm eye and inside to wrist measure added, dot on this line where the diameter begins and make dot A, take half the space between dot A and end of line 1 and make a dot, one-fourth inch to the left of this dot make dot B, to the left of dot A make dot C inside to bend measure.

2. Line 2 is two-thirds the arm eye measure.

3. Line 3 is the same length as line 1.

4. Draw lines 4, 5 and 6 from dots B, A and C to line 3.

5. On line 5, one-half inch from dot A, make dot D; three-fourths of an inch from D make dot E.

6. On line 6, one and one-half inches from dot C, make dot F; three-fourths of an inch from dot F make dot G; and draw a line from D to F and E to G; and one inch above line 1 at bottom of sleeve make dot H, and draw line from F to H.

7. Draw line 7 three-fourths the wrist measure straight down from end of line 1; and three inches to the left of the end of line 7 make a dot and draw line 8 from H to dot just made.

8. On line 8 make dot K, three-fourths the wrist measure from dot H; two inches inside of H make dot I, and from I, one-fourth the wrist measure, mark J.

9. Dot L is one inch above line 3 on line 2. From L draw a line straight to line 4 and make dot M. Dot N is one-half the space between lines 1 and 3 on line 2; draw line from N to line 4 and make dot O.

10. On line 6, inside of F, mark for the elbow so that the upper sleeve is three inches wider than the under sleeve. Mark R for upper sleeve from F, and Q for under sleeve from G.

11.   Take tape measure and place shoulder measure on dot
N and measure for elbow, letting tape pass line 6, between Q
and R; make a dot where your neck to elbow measure comes
to : then draw line 9 from F through dot just made to line 3,
and mark Q and R on this line.

12.   Draw a line from M to R and from O to Q last made.
and from R to K, and from Q to J. and from G to I.

13.   Curve top of under sleeve from E to O. and curve
inside of upper sleeve from D to F and F to H, and curve
inside of under sleeve from E to G and from G to I. In
curving the top of upper sleeve begin at D and curve to one-
quarter inch below dot N to line 2. and to one-half inch below
dot M on line 4. and measure for upper, middle and lower arms
and curve outside of sleeve according to measure.

P. S.—The front seam of the sleeve is sewed in where the
back shoulder line crosses line 6 on line 2, the back seam half
the width of side body ; always make the sleeve from one to
one and one-half inches larger than the arm eye.

———— •

SKIRT DRAFT.
COPYRIGHTED.

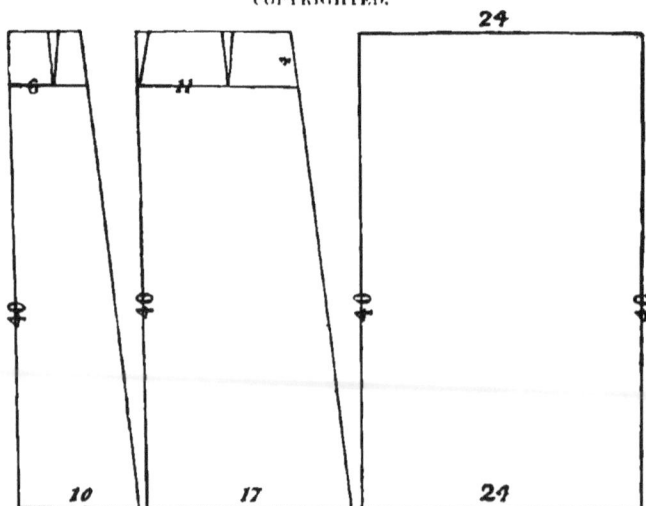

SLEEVE No. 2.

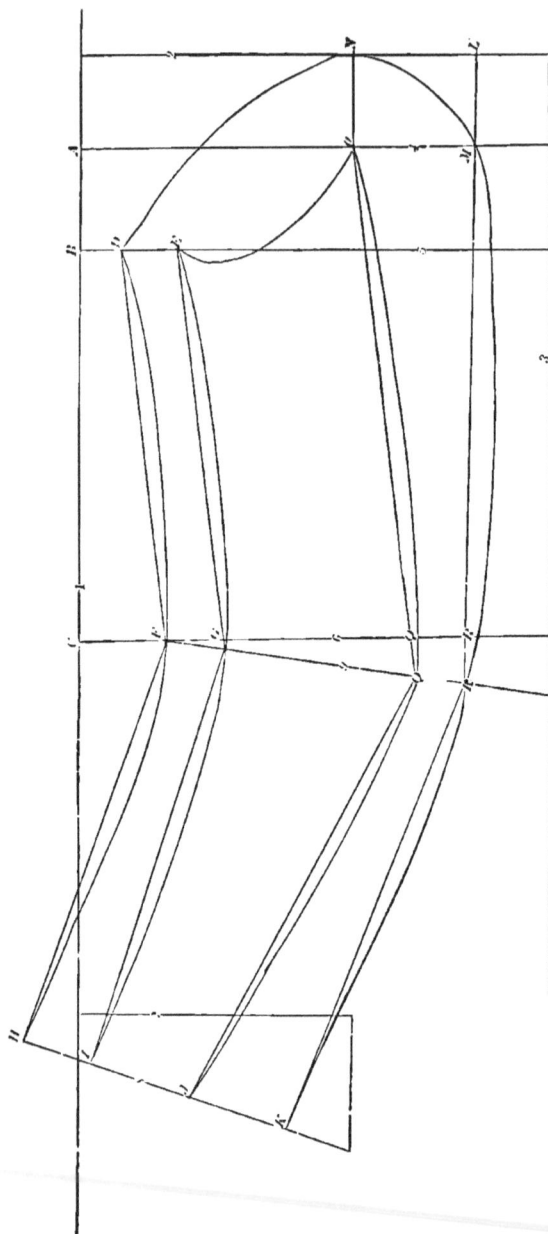

Measure for Drafting Sleeve.

1.—Arm Eye . . . . 14 inches	6.—Upper Arm . . . . 12 inches
2.—Neck to Elbow . . . . 19½ inches	7.—Middle Arm . . . . 11 inches
3.—Shoulder . . . . 4½ inches	8.—Elbow . . . . 11 inches
4.—Inside to Bend . . . . 8 inches	9.—Lower Arm . . . . 10 inches
5.—Inside to Wrist . . . . 16 inches	10.—Wrist . . . . 8 inches

Rules for Drafting Sleeve No. 2.

1. Line 1 is the diameter of arm eye and inside to wrist measure added, dot on this line where the diameter begins and make dot B, take half the space between dot B and end of line 1 and make a dot. one-fourth inch to the right of this dot make dot A. to the left of dot B make dot C inside to bend measure.

2. Line 2 is two-thirds the arm-eye measure.

3. Line 3 is the same length as line 1.

4. Draw lines 4, 5 and 6 from dots A, B and C to line 3.

5. On line 5. one-half inch from dot B. make dot D ; three-fourths of an inch from D make dot E.

6. On line 6. one and three-fourth inches from dot C. make dot F ; three-fourths of an inch from dot F make dot G ; and draw a line from D to F and E to G ; and one inch above line 1 at bottom of sleeve make dot H, and draw line from F to H.

7. Draw line 7 three-fourths the wrist measure straight down from end of line 1 ; and three inches to the left of the end of line 7 make a dot and draw line 8 from dot H to dot just made.

8. On line 8 make dot K, three-fourths the wrist measure from dot H ; two inches inside of H make dot I, and from I, one-fourth the wrist measure. mark J.

9. Dot L is one and one-half inches above line 3 on line 2. From L draw a line straight to line 4 and make dot M. Dot N is one-third the space from L to end of line 1 and draw line from N to line 4 and make dot O.

10. On line 6. inside of F, mark for the elbow so that the upper sleeve is two inches wider than the under sleeve. Mark R for upper sleeve from F, and Q for under sleeve from G.

11. Take tape measure and place shoulder measure on dot N and measure for elbow, letting tape pass line 6 between Q and R; make a dot where your neck to elbow measure comes to; then draw line 9 from F, through dot just made, to line 3, and mark Q and R on this line.

12. Draw a line from M to R, and from O to Q last made, and from R to K, and from Q to J, and G to I.

13. Curve top of under sleeve from E to O, and curve inside of upper sleeve from D to F and from F to H, and curve inside of under sleeve from E to G and from G to I. In curving the top of upper sleeve begin at D and curve to N and to M, and measure for upper, middle and lower arms, and curve outside of sleeve according to measure.

•

For Misses or Children.

Proceed as in Basque No. 1, until you get to Rule 18.

18. Measure the space between lines 6 and 7 on slanting waist line, for darts, in four equal parts. The space between darts is found by measuring three-eighths of an inch on each side of the centre mark.

19. Draw centre line of dart from the centre of space the height of dart and slant back one-fourth inch, then use long curvature from the top of the line to the centre of each dart, which will give the desired fullness for one dart.

20. One and one-fourth inches to the left of dot A on waist line make dot B, then take half the space between dot A and line 5, and make dot C on waist line. Place large end of curvature at dot B and draw a curve line to dot F, for inside of back. Use curvature the same way from dot C, letting it touch back line at line 2 for outside of side body.

21. To find the back line of the front and width of side body, measure from B to A and from front curved line to dart, omitting the width of dart, and then from back of dart, to half the waist measure and make dot on waist line.

22. Take half the space between this dot and back of dart and make dot H, dot D is the same distance to the right of H as the waist measure is from C. Draw line 12 from H up to arm eye half the space between lines 5 and 6, draw line 13 from D up to top of line 12.

23. Extend lines 4 and 7 to the bottom of paper and centre line of dart, also outside line of dart leaving one-half inch space each side of centre line.

24. Measure for hip line on lines 7 and 4 : from line 1 the height of hip and draw line 14 for hip line.

25. Mark dots B. C. D and H on hip line.

26. Draw back line from A to one-half inch to the left of end of line 4 at bottom of paper with rule.

27. Draw inside of back from B straight down to bottom of paper with rule.

28. Back of the side body is sloped from C one inch to the right of C on hip line.

29. Front of side body is sloped from D two inches to the left of D on hip line.

30. Back of front is sloped from H two inches to the right of H on hip line.

31. If too large or too small after measuring all the places on hip line. add on or take off to suit the hip measure.

BLAZER COAT AND VEST.

COPYRIGHTED.

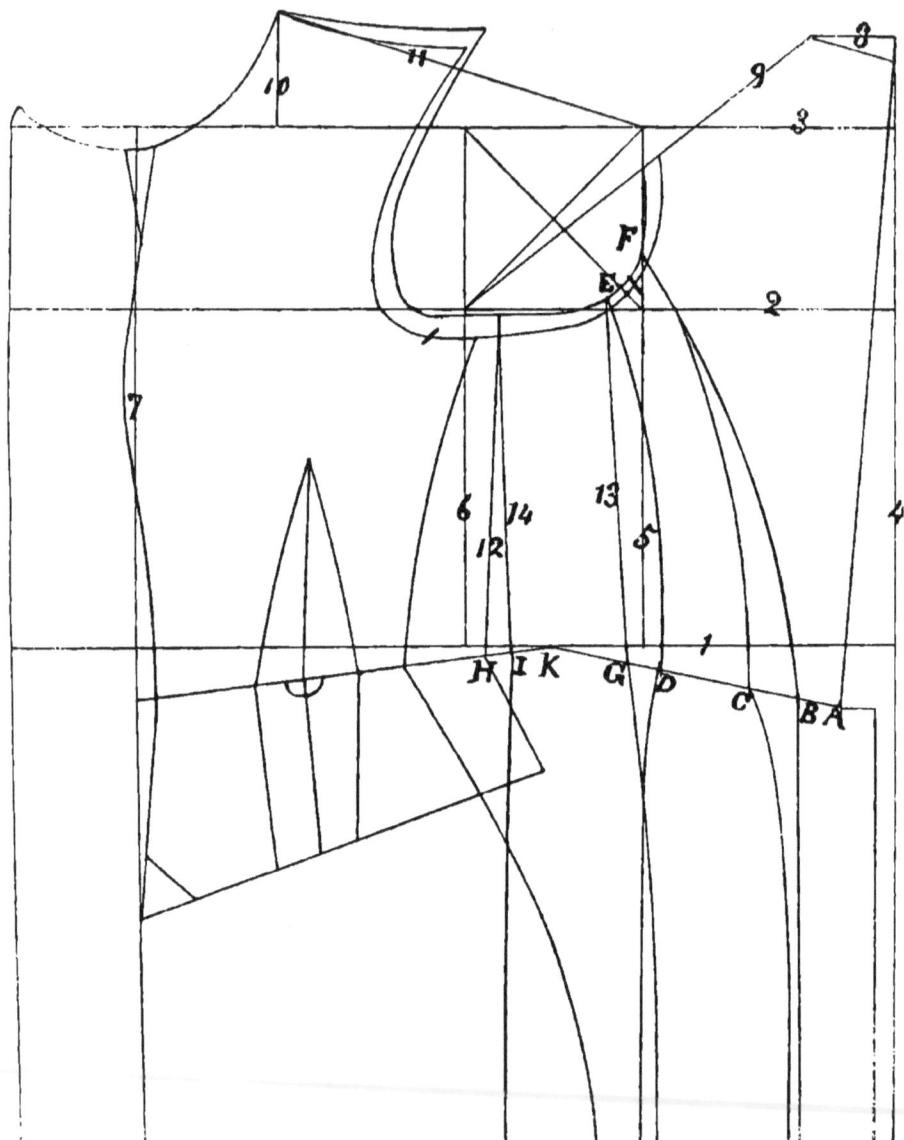

Blazer Coat and Vest.

Proceed as in Basque No. 1, for Blazer coat and vest with the exception of the following changes :

Draw line one 14 inches from bottom of paper for belt-line.

Draw line 2 one-half inch higher than under arm measure.

Dot [A] is one and one-half inches to the left of end of line 4.

After getting arm-eye same as dress, then make back and front shoulder lines one-quarter inch shorter than curve coat-arm-eye around to one inch below junction of lines 2 and 6, which makes coat-arm-eye large enough to go over the dress.

Put one Dart in vest-front.

Find Dot [G] and [H] the same as in Basque No. 1.

Dot to the left of line 7 on lines 3 and 1 one-fourth the neck measure, and draw line from one-half inch above line 3 through dots just made down to bottom of paper, which makes front of coat, and curve neck to top of this line above line 3.

Put in one-half inch dart at neck on line 7, as shown in draft.

Three-fourth inch to the left of end of line 12, in arm-eye make a [dot.] Then measure the width of the dart at waist line and put the same space to the left of [H] and make a [dot,] use small end of curvature at dot in arm-eye, to [dot] at waist line, which makes back of the front of coat.

Then measure under arm—side body and back, and from front of coat to half the hip measure, then use curvature from back of front coat on waist line to bottom of paper as shown in draft.

DOUBLE-BREASTED COAT.

Will be explained by Teacher.

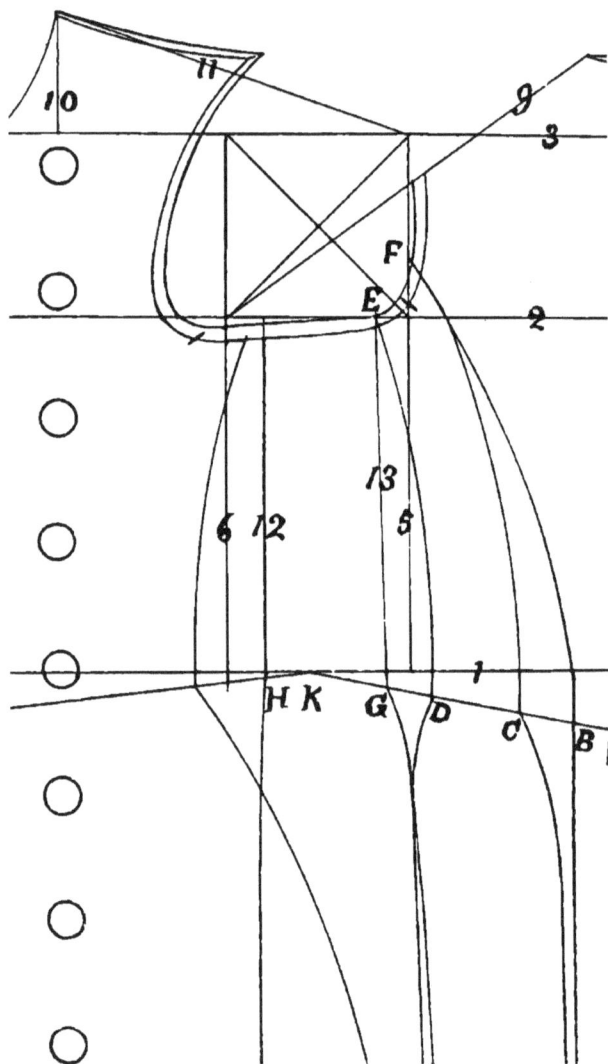